INTERSECTIONAL ECHOES

Feminism from the Margins

By

Lillian J. Robbins

Copyright © 2024 Lillian J. Robbins

The content of this book is protected by copyright. Reproduction or transmission of any part of this book, whether through electronic or mechanical means, including photocopying, recording, or any information storage and retrieval system, is prohibited without written permission from the copyright owner. This workbook is intended to provide general information on the topics covered and should not be considered as a substitute for professional or legal advice. If you require expert assistance, it is recommended that you seek the services of a qualified professional.

Table of contents

Table of contents 3
Introduction 7
CHAPTER 1 11
   The Origins of Intersectionality 11
CHAPTER 2 16
   The Problem with the Mainstream Movement 16
CHAPTER 3 22
   Voices from the Hood: Feminism in Marginalized Communities 22
CHAPTER 4 28
   Economic Oppression: The Silent Barrier 28
      The Wage Gap Isn't Equal for All Women .. 28
      Education: The Mirage of Opportunity 30
      Invisible Labor and Unpaid Work 31
      Class as a Feminist Issue 32
      Grassroots Feminism: Fighting Economic Oppression 33
CHAPTER 5 35
   The Weight of Culture and Tradition 35
      Patriarchy in the Cloak of Tradition 35
      The Struggle Between Identity and Oppression 37
      Global Perspectives: Patriarchal Norms Across Borders 39
      The Path Forward: Navigating Cultural

Feminism 41
Reclaiming the Narrative.......................... 43

CHAPTER 6 45
Beyond Gender: Sexuality and Queer Feminism ... 45
Sexuality and Gender Identity: A Complex Intersection 46
The Struggles of LGBTQ+ Individuals in Feminism 48
Queer Feminism: Centering Sexuality and Identity 51
From Exclusion to Inclusion: Building an Inclusive Feminism 53
Embracing a Queer Feminist Future 55

CHAPTER 7 57
Feminism in Crisis: Conflict Zones and Displacement 57
Women at the Epicenter of Crisis 58
The Role of Women as Agents of Change . 60
Displacement and Feminism: A Double Burden 62
Women as Global Feminist Leaders 64
Connecting Global Struggles with Feminist Principles 66
Feminism's Global Duty 67

CHAPTER 8 69
Health Disparities: Fighting for Bodily Autonomy.... 69
The Crisis of Maternal Mortality 70
The Battle for Abortion Rights 72
Mental Health: The Silent Struggle 74
Bodily Autonomy: The Feminist Demand for Health Equity... 76

The Intersection of Health and Feminism ..78

CHAPTER 9 80

The Power of Representation 80

- The Narrow Lens of Mainstream Representation...81
- Breaking the Silence: Diverse Voices in Feminism 84
- Media's Role in Shaping Feminist Narratives 86
- The Importance of Authentic Feminist Representation...88
- Conclusion: The Power of Representation in Shaping Feminist Futures 90

CHAPTER 10 91

Feminism and Allyship: Bridging Divides...............92

- Understanding Allyship: More Than Just Support 93
- The Dangers of "Performative" Allyship 95
- The Role of Privileged Women in Feminist Activism...96
- Practical Ways to Practice Allyship.............98
- Allyship as Solidarity in Action 102
- A Feminist Movement of Solidarity 103

CHAPTER 11 105

Grassroots Initiatives: Revolution from the Ground Up 105

- The Power of Community-Based Feminism 106
- Case Studies of Successful Grassroots Feminist Movements..................................108
- Feminism from the Margins: The Role of Marginalized Women in Grassroots

  Movements 111
  How to Support or Start a Grassroots
  Feminist Initiative 114
  Building Feminist Movements from the
  Ground Up 116
Chapter 12 .... **118**
  Building an Inclusive Future................................ 118
  Key Lessons from the Book 119
  The Future of Feminism............................ 128
  Conclusion 129

Introduction

The word "feminism" carries with it both power and controversy—a rallying cry for change, yet, at times, a source of division. As feminism has evolved over decades, so too have its blind spots, leaving behind a trail of voices unheard, stories untold, and battles unrecognized. At the heart of this evolution lies a sobering truth: feminism, as powerful and transformative as it is, has not always been inclusive.

Intersectional feminism challenges this imbalance, urging us to reconsider the lens through which we view women's struggles. Coined by Kimberlé Crenshaw, intersectionality emphasizes that the experiences of women at the margins—those navigating the intersecting barriers of race, class, sexuality, ability, and beyond—cannot be disentangled from their gender. It is within these intersections that the most profound truths of oppression and resilience reside.

To truly reclaim feminism, we must move beyond the narratives that dominate mainstream discourse. The struggles of a Black single mother navigating systemic racism while striving for economic survival are not the same as those of a middle-class white woman fighting for workplace equity. Both stories matter, but they must be told in ways that honor their distinct realities.

Intersectional feminism is not just a theory; it is a call to action. It demands that we widen the scope of our understanding, amplifying the echoes of those who have been pushed to the periphery. These echoes, though faint, carry a transformative power. They force us to reckon with uncomfortable truths, to dismantle the hierarchies within feminism itself, and to imagine a movement that leaves no one behind.

But let us be clear: this book is not a critique for the sake of criticism. It is an offer to extend our horizons and a challenge.. By listening to these echoes—by centering the marginalized, the silenced, and the overlooked—we create a feminism that reflects the diversity of the human experience.

As you journey through the pages of this work, prepare to step into unfamiliar terrain. You will meet voices that challenge the status quo, stories that demand your attention, and ideas that may unsettle you. This is the essence of intersectional feminism: it does not seek comfort; it seeks justice.

So let us begin—not from the center, but from the margins. It is there, in the places often ignored, that the future of feminism is waiting to be heard.

CHAPTER 1

The Origins of Intersectionality

The word "intersectionality" may feel like a modern buzzword, but its roots stretch deep into the intertwined struggles of race, class, and gender. To understand where it began, we must journey back to the late 20th century, where the framework of intersectionality emerged from the cracks in mainstream feminist and civil rights movements—spaces that failed to address the unique burdens borne by women of color.

In 1989, legal scholar and activist Kimberlé Crenshaw coined the term "intersectionality." At its core, the concept was deceptively simple: it highlighted how systems of oppression overlap, creating compounded disadvantages for individuals who exist at the crossroads of multiple identities. Crenshaw used the term to critique how both feminist theory and antiracist movements often excluded Black women, leaving their experiences invisible in discussions that claimed to fight for liberation.

Imagine, for a moment, standing at a literal intersection. One road signifies race, the other gender. If you are a Black woman, the traffic from both directions doesn't just meet—it collides, amplifying the chaos and risk. Crenshaw's work illuminated this reality, showing how Black women are often left stranded at these intersections, unprotected by the frameworks designed to address only one dimension of their identities.

Historically, this erasure is not new. Black women like Sojourner Truth and Anna Julia Cooper had long pointed out that the feminist and abolitionist movements of their time failed to recognize the unique challenges faced by women who lived at the nexus of race and gender oppression. Truth's famous question, "Ain't I a Woman?" was not rhetorical; it was a demand to be seen, to be heard, and to be included.

Crenshaw's framework was groundbreaking because it provided a language for what many marginalized women had long understood but struggled to articulate. It drew attention to cases like those of Black women workers whose legal claims of discrimination were dismissed because their experiences did not neatly fit into the categories of "racism" or "sexism." For them, the law failed to see that their oppression was both—and more.

But intersectionality is more than a critique; it is a lens, a way of understanding how power operates in society. It challenges the simplicity of single-axis thinking, where gender, race, or class is examined in isolation. Instead, it insists that we consider how these systems interact to shape lived experiences.

For example, a low-income Latina immigrant faces challenges that cannot be reduced to her gender alone. Her struggles with economic instability, cultural prejudice, and immigration status are all interconnected. Ignoring this complexity not only diminishes her reality but also weakens the fight for justice. Intersectionality reminds us that oppression is not a one-size-fits-all phenomenon—it is layered, nuanced, and deeply personal.

As we delve into the history and implications of intersectionality, it becomes clear that this framework is not a mere academic exercise. It is a call to action. It demands that feminism expand its scope, embracing the voices of those whose lives sit at the crossroads of marginalization. Without this, any movement for liberation remains incomplete.

Intersectionality, then, is not just a theory—it is a mirror. It reflects the limitations of traditional feminist and social justice efforts while offering a path toward a more inclusive and equitable future. To build that future, we must begin by acknowledging the intersections in our own lives and in the lives of others. Only then can we hope to create a world where everyone's story is heard, and no one is left behind.

CHAPTER 2

The Problem with the Mainstream Movement

Mainstream feminism has often worn the face of progress, but beneath its surface lies a troubling truth: its focus has largely centered on the experiences of middle-class, white women. While this narrow lens has brought victories like voting rights, workplace equality, and reproductive freedoms, it has also come at a cost—a feminism that excludes far too many.

The cracks in the foundation of the mainstream movement began to show early. First-wave feminism, with its iconic suffragette marches, was heralded as a fight for all women, but the reality was far more exclusive. Black women were not only sidelined but explicitly excluded from many suffrage campaigns. Figures like Ida B. Wells and Mary Church Terrell had to fight for inclusion in movements that supposedly championed "universal" rights.

Even in its second wave, mainstream feminism failed to account for the diverse realities of women's lives. Betty Friedan's *The Feminine Mystique* famously described the malaise of middle-class housewives but ignored the labor of working-class women, particularly women of color, whose struggles weren't about escaping the home but surviving in it. The movement's demands for workplace equality and sexual liberation were often framed in terms that presumed white, heterosexual, able-bodied norms—leaving behind women who faced intersecting oppressions.

This exclusion wasn't just oversight; it had tangible consequences. Women of color, LGBTQ+ individuals, disabled women, and others were forced to create their own spaces and movements, such as the Combahee River

Collective, which declared in 1977 that Liberating Black women would require tearing down all repressive structures, which would then guarantee freedom for everyone else.

Mainstream feminism's narrow focus also perpetuate harmful stereotypes. By centering the struggles of a privileged few, it ignored the complex realities of marginalized groups. For instance, white feminism often framed sexual harassment and assault through the lens of corporate workplaces, ignoring the experiences of immigrant women in domestic labor or undocumented women in agriculture. Similarly, reproductive rights campaigns often spotlighted abortion access while neglecting issues like forced sterilization, which disproportionately affected Indigenous, Black, and disabled women.

This "one-size-fits-all" feminism has long-term consequences. It fosters resentment and mistrust between groups, making it harder to build coalitions. It also reinforces the idea that feminism is a monolith—an agenda that serves only those who already hold certain privileges.

For LGBTQ+ individuals, mainstream feminism's emphasis on binary gender roles often leaves little room for their experiences. Trans women, in particular, have faced outright hostility from some feminist spaces, a stance that ignores the unique violence and discrimination they face. Similarly, disabled women often find their struggles erased in conversations about body autonomy and workplace equality. How can a movement claim to fight for equality while overlooking so many?

The problem with mainstream feminism isn't just who it excludes—it's also how it excludes. By failing to listen to and uplift marginalized voices, it perpetuates the very hierarchies it claims to dismantle. Feminism cannot succeed if it replicates systems of power and privilege within its own ranks.

What's the solution? It starts with recognizing that feminism cannot be a single narrative. It must be a mosaic, where each piece represents the unique struggles and triumphs of women across all intersections. True liberation demands a movement that understands and addresses the ways race, class, gender identity, sexuality, ability, and more intersect to shape oppression.

Critiquing mainstream feminism is not an act of division but one of accountability. By addressing its blind spots, the movement can become what it has always claimed to be: a fight for *all* women. The future of feminism depends on this reckoning—on a willingness to listen, learn, and make space for those who have been silenced. Only then can feminism fulfill its promise of equality and justice.

CHAPTER 3

Voices from the Hood: Feminism in Marginalized Communities

Feminism, in its purest form, has always been about resilience—about pushing back against systems that dehumanize and diminish. Nowhere is this resilience more vivid than in the neighborhoods often dismissed or overlooked by mainstream feminism. In these spaces—where survival itself is a daily act of defiance—women are crafting a feminism that is raw, rooted, and revolutionary.

The term "hood feminism" isn't just a catchy phrase; it's a lifeline. It's the acknowledgment that feminism doesn't start in academia or legislative halls but in the kitchens, classrooms, and community centers where women fight for their families, their dignity, and their futures.

These women don't wait for think tanks to validate their struggles or for polished campaigns to amplify their voices. They take action because they must.

Consider the story of Marisol, a single mother living in East Los Angeles. By day, she juggles two part-time jobs, but by night, she transforms her tiny apartment into a sanctuary for teenage girls in her neighborhood. These are young women facing everything from gang violence to food insecurity. For Marisol, feminism isn't about grand gestures; it's about providing a hot meal, a listening ear, and a reminder that their lives matter.

Or take Fatimah, a hijabi woman in Detroit who started a literacy program for young mothers. Her initiative began after she noticed that many women in her community were struggling to navigate housing applications and healthcare forms. Fatimah's work isn't often labeled as "feminism," but that's exactly what it is:

empowering women to reclaim agency over their lives.

In marginalized communities, feminism is deeply intertwined with survival. It's not about the theoretical; it's about the practical. Grassroots efforts to fight for better schools, safer streets, and affordable healthcare are acts of feminist advocacy, even if they don't come with hashtags or media coverage. These are the battles that mainstream feminism often overlooks in its pursuit of more palatable issues.

Hood feminism also challenges the sanitized narratives that dominate mainstream spaces. In these communities, feminism isn't neat or polished—it's messy, fierce, and unapologetic. It recognizes that the struggles of women cannot be separated from the struggles of their communities. It's a feminism that sees the fight against police brutality as a feminist issue because Black mothers are losing their sons to systemic violence. It sees housing discrimination as a feminist issue because women are disproportionately affected by eviction and homelessness.

What makes hood feminism so powerful is its ability to adapt and persevere. These communities don't have the luxury of waiting for systemic change; they create their own systems of support. When shelters are full, women open their homes. When schools fail their children, they organize tutoring circles. When elected officials ignore their needs, they run for office themselves.

This isn't to romanticize struggle or to suggest that these women are content to fight alone. Rather, it's to highlight the ingenuity and tenacity that emerge when systems fail. Feminism in marginalized communities isn't a response to privilege—it's a rejection of neglect.

But hood feminism isn't just reactive; it's transformative. It offers lessons for the broader feminist movement about what true inclusivity looks like. It's a reminder that feminism doesn't have to be perfect to be powerful, that it doesn't need to come from glossy platforms to matter.

To truly embrace feminism, we must listen to these voices—not as a gesture of solidarity but as an act of accountability. The narratives of women like Marisol and Fatimah are not side stories; they are the story. They are proof that feminism thrives in unexpected places, that it is alive and evolving in the margins.

As we move forward, we must ask ourselves: How can we amplify these voices without co-opting them? How can we learn from their struggles without patronizing their strength? The answers lie in humility, in recognizing that mainstream feminism has much to learn from the hood.

Feminism doesn't belong to the privileged few; it belongs to every woman who has ever said, "Enough." And in the hood, that declaration isn't just words—it's a way of life.

CHAPTER 4

Economic Oppression: The Silent Barrier

Economic inequality is the quiet force that shapes countless lives, particularly for women in marginalized communities. It does not announce itself with dramatic flair, yet its effects are deeply felt—threading through their choices, opportunities, and futures. This chapter explores how economic oppression intersects with gender, creating a silent but insurmountable barrier that demands feminism's urgent attention.

The Wage Gap Isn't Equal for All Women

The wage gap has long been a rallying cry for feminist movements. The phrase "women earn 77 cents to a man's dollar" is frequently repeated, but this statistic conceals an uncomfortable truth. The disparity is far worse for women of color Black women earn around 64 cents, while Latina women average just 57 cents. These disparities don't stem from individual failings but from systemic inequalities that compound along lines of race, gender, and class.

For women in marginalized communities, low wages mean more than financial frustration—they mean hard choices: paying rent or feeding their children, seeking medical care or saving for emergencies. These decisions reflect the daily reality of living on the edge, where every cent counts. Meanwhile, mainstream feminism often focuses on boardrooms and glass ceilings, ignoring the millions of women who will never even see the door to those rooms.

Education: The Mirage of Opportunity

Education is often presented as the key to upward mobility, but for many women, particularly those in underprivileged areas, it's a promise that doesn't always hold. Access to quality education remains out of reach for communities facing systemic disinvestment. Schools in poorer neighborhoods are underfunded and overcrowded, offering fewer resources and limited pathways to success.

For young women, these barriers are only the beginning. College, hailed as the gateway to better prospects, comes with insurmountable costs. Many take on massive student loans, only to graduate into a workforce that undervalues their contributions. Others can't afford to attend at all, sacrificing education for immediate financial needs. This cycle ensures that economic oppression is passed down, with little room for escape.

Invisible Labor and Unpaid Work

Economic oppression isn't confined to paychecks and promotions. Women, particularly in marginalized communities, shoulder the brunt of unpaid labor—caring for children, maintaining households, and supporting extended families. This invisible work, while crucial to the functioning of society, goes unrecognized and uncompensated.

Consider Maria, a single mother living in a low-income neighborhood. Her day starts before sunrise, preparing her kids for school and working a physically demanding job that barely covers the bills. Afterward, she spends hours cooking, cleaning, and helping her children with homework. Maria's labor keeps her family afloat, but the lack of economic support means she's always one unexpected expense away from crisis.

This unpaid labor underscores a critical flaw in how society measures value. If feminism doesn't address the economic contributions women make outside formal employment, it risks ignoring a significant aspect of gender inequality.

Class as a Feminist Issue

Class-based disparities are often treated as secondary in feminist discourse, but for millions of women, they are the central issue. A single mother struggling to afford childcare or a young woman unable to escape a low-paying job doesn't have the luxury of thinking about abstract feminist ideals. For her, survival takes precedence.

Yet, class and gender are inseparable. Economic dependence limits women's ability to leave abusive relationships, pursue education, or advocate for their rights. Feminism must recognize that true equality isn't just about breaking glass ceilings—it's about breaking down the structural barriers that keep so many women trapped.

Grassroots Feminism: Fighting Economic Oppression

While mainstream feminism often overlooks class issues, grassroots movements in marginalized communities are leading the charge. These women aren't waiting for systemic change—they're creating it themselves. From mutual aid networks to worker cooperatives, they are finding ways to support one another and challenge economic injustice.

One such example is the National Domestic Workers Alliance, which advocates for fair wages and legal protections for women in caregiving roles. These efforts may not make headlines, but they are vital in pushing for an inclusive feminism that addresses economic oppression.

Economic oppression may not be as visible as other forms of inequality, but its impact is just as devastating. Feminism must broaden its lens to include the struggles of women facing financial hardship. This means advocating for policies like living wages, affordable childcare, and equitable access to education. It means recognizing that the fight for gender equality is also a fight against poverty.

The silent barrier of economic oppression cannot remain in the shadows. By addressing class-based disparities head-on, feminism can become a movement that truly uplifts all women, leaving no one behind.

CHAPTER 5

The Weight of Culture and Tradition

Culture is a living, breathing thing. It shapes our identities, guides our values, and informs the way we navigate the world. But when culture is woven with patriarchal threads, it can become a suffocating force that limits women's freedom. The weight of tradition bears heavily on the lives of women across the globe, often dictating their choices, behavior, and even their worth. This chapter explores how cultural and traditional expectations impact women's freedom, examining the delicate balance between embracing cultural identity and resisting oppressive norms.

Patriarchy in the Cloak of Tradition

In many societies, patriarchy is not just a social structure—it is embedded in tradition, passed down from one generation to the next. This patriarchal influence can be seen in customs, religious practices, and societal roles that shape a woman's place in the world. From the very beginning, girls are taught their worth is tied to family, honor, and obedience. These cultural expectations often restrict their autonomy, shaping their lives in ways that limit their potential.

Take, for example, the practice of child marriage, still prevalent in parts of South Asia and Sub-Saharan Africa. Girls as young as 10 or 12 are often married off in the name of tradition, family honor, or economic necessity. While some argue that these customs are part of long-standing cultural practices, the reality is that they are a direct manifestation of patriarchal control. These young girls, denied agency over their own bodies and futures, face a lifetime of inequality, often compounded by limited access to education, economic independence, and personal freedom.

In these contexts, tradition becomes a tool of subjugation, reinforcing gendered roles that place women in a perpetual state of dependence and vulnerability. But it's important to recognize that not all cultural practices are inherently oppressive. Many cultural traditions are deeply connected to identity and community, and the challenge lies in discerning which aspects are worth preserving and which are harmful.

The Struggle Between Identity and Oppression

Cultural feminism seeks to reconcile these two forces—honoring cultural identity while challenging harmful traditions. It is a delicate balance. In some societies, rejecting cultural norms that are tied to gender inequality can be seen as an act of betrayal, a rejection of one's heritage. Women who attempt to break free from these traditions may face backlash not only from men but also from their own communities, who view such acts as undermining the very fabric of their culture.

Yet, true empowerment cannot be realized when women are shackled by practices that limit their freedom. Navigating this tension is complicated. Feminists in these contexts must ask: How do we honor our cultural heritage while dismantling the patriarchal elements that have embedded themselves within it?

Take, for example, the practice of female genital mutilation (FGM), a deeply entrenched tradition in many African and Middle Eastern countries. While FGM is often defended as a cultural or religious practice, it is rooted in patriarchal control over women's bodies. Women who speak out against FGM are often vilified, but many grassroots activists have shown that it is possible to challenge such traditions while still respecting cultural values. Through community dialogue, education, and local empowerment, the practice is being slowly eradicated in some regions, without erasing cultural identity.

This example illustrates a broader point: feminism can coexist with cultural practices, but only when those practices do not infringe on the basic rights and freedoms of women. Cultural feminism calls for a reevaluation of traditions that perpetuate inequality and seeks to replace them with practices that empower and uplift women.

Global Perspectives: Patriarchal Norms Across Borders

The impact of culture on women's freedom is not confined to any one region. Patriarchal norms are a global issue, reinforced through various cultural lenses, each with its own set of expectations. In the Western world, for example, the pressure to conform to beauty standards can be just as limiting as traditional gender roles in other parts of the world. The commodification of women's bodies in media and advertising presents a form of cultural oppression that limits women's autonomy over how they present themselves and what they can achieve.

In the Middle East, the dress code for women is often dictated by both religious and cultural norms, which can severely restrict their mobility and social participation. While there is significant debate about the role of religion in these practices, many women have found ways to reinterpret religious texts and challenge restrictive laws without forsaking their faith. The challenge, as in other regions, is not to eradicate culture or tradition, but to reframe them in a way that allows for equality and freedom.

The global struggle of women against cultural and traditional norms reveals one undeniable truth: patriarchy is adaptable. It doesn't simply exist in one form or location—it morphs to fit the cultural context. Whether through dress codes, beauty standards, marriage expectations, or even domestic roles, patriarchy hides behind the veil of culture, perpetuating inequality in countless ways.

The Path Forward: Navigating Cultural Feminism

So how do we navigate this complex terrain? How do we engage in feminism without erasing the very identities that have shaped us? The answer lies in a process of reclamation and transformation. Rather than discarding cultural practices altogether, we must critically engage with them, asking which ones serve women's empowerment and which ones reinforce patriarchal power structures.

Feminism must encourage the reinvention of tradition. It is possible to reclaim cultural practices and reinterpret them in ways that prioritize equality. A feminist approach to culture involves active participation in community dialogue, creating spaces for women to voice their concerns and reshape the practices that affect them.

An example of this transformative approach can be seen in the work of indigenous women across the Americas. Many indigenous communities have traditions of matriarchy, where women hold significant roles in decision-making and leadership. These cultures have long upheld the dignity and power of women, but colonization has sought to undermine these practices. Today, indigenous women are reclaiming their cultural spaces, revitalizing their communities, and asserting their rightful place in society.

Feminism from the margins requires this same spirit of reclamation and transformation. Women from marginalized communities must be empowered to take ownership of their cultural identities while also breaking free from the oppressive traditions that limit their potential. This is not about rejecting culture or identity, but about reclaiming them in a way that frees women from the weight of harmful traditions.

Conclusion: Reclaiming the Narrative

Cultural feminism is not about erasing the past—it's about rewriting the narrative. Women in marginalized communities deserve the space to define their own identities, free from the constraints of patriarchal expectations. By challenging cultural norms and transforming traditions, we can create a feminist movement that respects both the past and the future, without sacrificing freedom for identity.

The weight of culture and tradition may be heavy, but it is not unmovable. With resilience, dialogue, and reclamation, women can reclaim their cultural spaces, shaping their own futures while honoring their heritage.

CHAPTER 6

Beyond Gender: Sexuality and Queer Feminism

Feminism, at its core, is about dismantling oppressive systems that limit freedom, autonomy, and equality. Yet, the feminist movement itself has not always been inclusive of all women, let alone those whose identities fall outside traditional gender norms. As the feminist movement has evolved, it has become clear that it must go beyond gender to truly address the intersectional issues that affect the most marginalized within our society. This chapter explores the intersection of sexual orientation, gender identity, and feminism, focusing on the challenges faced by LGBTQ+ individuals within and outside feminist movements, and advocating for a more inclusive feminism that acknowledges the diversity of human experience.

Sexuality and Gender Identity: A Complex Intersection

Gender is often perceived as a binary concept—male or female, masculine or feminine. But for many people, this binary framework does not capture the complexity of their identities. Queer individuals, who do not fit neatly into these categories, face a world that is constantly trying to categorize and define them. Feminism, traditionally centered on women's rights, must expand to recognize that the issues affecting queer and transgender individuals are also rooted in gendered oppression. The struggle for equality is not just a battle between men and women, but one that includes the entire spectrum of gender and sexual identities.

Transgender and non-binary individuals face unique challenges that are often invisible to the mainstream feminist movement. Trans women, for example, face the dual oppression of being both women and transgender, often experiencing discrimination not only from patriarchal systems but also from within the feminist movement itself. Transphobia, both systemic and interpersonal, is a painful reality for many in the LGBTQ+ community. Yet, despite these challenges, queer and transgender people have long been involved in feminist activism, fighting for visibility, rights, and recognition.

This chapter aims to shed light on the intersection of sexuality and gender identity within feminism, highlighting the ways in which traditional feminist frameworks must be adapted to reflect a broader, more inclusive understanding of gender and sexuality.

The Struggles of LGBTQ+ Individuals in Feminism

While many feminist movements claim to be progressive, there is often a tension between the mainstream feminist agenda and the struggles of LGBTQ+ individuals. This tension arises in part from the fact that much of the feminist movement has historically been dominated by cisgender, heterosexual women, who may not fully understand the unique challenges faced by those whose gender and sexual identities fall outside the traditional binary.

One major point of contention has been the feminist critique of the male gaze and the objectification of women. While these are vital issues, feminist discourse sometimes neglects the unique objectification and marginalization faced by LGBTQ+ individuals. Queer people, particularly trans women and gender-nonconforming individuals, often face not only sexual objectification but also violence, erasure, and stigmatization in ways that cisgender women do not.

Moreover, within the feminist movement, there are often struggles for inclusivity. Many trans women report feeling excluded from feminist spaces that prioritize cisgender women's experiences, while others may face outright rejection from feminist communities that are hostile to non-binary or transgender identities. This exclusion reinforces the very patriarchal structures feminism seeks to dismantle—by failing to acknowledge the fluidity of gender and sexuality, these movements perpetuate the same kind of restrictive, binary thinking they aim to oppose.

However, this is not to say that the feminist movement is without allies and advocates for the LGBTQ+ community. Many feminists—particularly those from more intersectional backgrounds—have long advocated for the inclusion of LGBTQ+ voices within feminist spaces. For these activists, feminism cannot claim to be truly liberatory unless it acknowledges the full spectrum of gender and sexual identities, and works to challenge all forms of gender-based oppression.

Queer Feminism: Centering Sexuality and Identity

Queer feminism is an emerging field that seeks to break free from traditional gender roles, and to create a feminism that is more inclusive of all identities, including those that exist outside the gender binary. At its heart, queer feminism challenges the idea that gender and sexuality should fit into fixed categories or be restricted by societal norms. Queer feminist thought is rooted in the belief that gender and sexuality are fluid, and that people should be free to express themselves in ways that are authentic to their own lived experiences.

For queer individuals, feminist movements have often offered both solidarity and tension. On the one hand, queer feminists share the broader feminist goals of gender equality and social justice; on the other, the traditional feminist framework—centered on cisgender, heterosexual women—has often excluded or marginalized their voices. Queer feminists argue that the feminist movement cannot move forward without addressing these exclusions, and that a truly inclusive feminist movement must recognize the full diversity of human experiences.

Queer feminism also challenges the traditional understanding of sexual violence, acknowledging that violence is not just something that happens to cisgender women at the hands of cisgender men. It explores the intersections of homophobia, transphobia, and misogyny, and addresses how these forms of violence manifest within LGBTQ+ communities. Queer feminism calls for a broader analysis of sexual violence that encompasses the experiences of all gender and sexual minorities.

From Exclusion to Inclusion: Building an Inclusive Feminism

The push for a more inclusive feminism is not just a matter of expanding the feminist tent to include LGBTQ+ individuals—it is about reimagining the feminist movement itself. It requires an understanding that gender and sexuality are not static; they are fluid, complex, and multifaceted. Feminism must be inclusive of all identities and sexualities, ensuring that people from all walks of life feel seen, heard, and valued.

To build a truly inclusive feminism, we must first center the voices of LGBTQ+ individuals in our conversations about oppression, equality, and justice. This means listening to the needs and experiences of queer and transgender people, and actively working to dismantle the barriers that have excluded them from feminist spaces. It also means critically examining the ways in which mainstream feminism has failed to address issues of gender identity and sexual orientation, and striving to create a more expansive framework that reflects the realities of all women and marginalized individuals.

As the feminist movement continues to evolve, it must recognize that a fight for gender equality cannot be limited to binary notions of gender. It must be a fight for the liberation of all people, regardless of their gender or sexual identity. True feminist solidarity is rooted in recognizing the dignity and humanity of every individual, and ensuring that all voices are heard in the struggle for freedom and justice.

Conclusion: Embracing a Queer Feminist Future

The future of feminism lies in its ability to adapt, grow, and be inclusive of all identities. Queer feminism provides a pathway forward, challenging traditional notions of gender and sexuality, and advocating for a world where everyone, regardless of gender or sexual identity, can live freely and authentically. As we build a more inclusive feminist movement, we must remember that the fight for gender equality is incomplete without the full inclusion of LGBTQ+ voices, experiences, and identities. Only by embracing all aspects of gender and sexuality can we truly build a feminism that is free from oppression and open to the richness of human diversity.

CHAPTER 7

Feminism in Crisis: Conflict Zones and Displacement

War, political instability, and displacement are forces that devastate societies, erode infrastructure, and upend entire communities. Yet, in the chaos of conflict, the resilience of women often shines through, despite the violence and instability that encircle them. This chapter delves into the unique challenges women face in crisis zones—whether in war-torn countries, refugee camps, or areas marked by political upheaval—and how these experiences intersect with feminist principles. While feminism often emphasizes the need for equality, freedom, and justice, these ideals take on new dimensions when applied to the lives of women living on the frontlines of global crises.

Women at the Epicenter of Crisis

In conflict zones and areas of political unrest, women are disproportionately affected by violence, displacement, and insecurity. They are often caught in the crossfire of war, subjected to gender-based violence, and forced into the roles of caregivers, survivors, and activists—all at once. Yet, their experiences are often ignored or sidelined in mainstream narratives of war, which are typically framed in terms of geopolitical struggles, military strategies, and state power.

Women in these regions face a multitude of dangers. In war-torn areas, they are at heightened risk of sexual violence, including rape as a weapon of war. In refugee camps, women often lack access to basic needs such as healthcare, education, and security, and are vulnerable to exploitation and trafficking. Displacement forces many women into desperate situations, where their rights are violated in both subtle and overt ways. Despite these challenges, women continue to demonstrate remarkable strength and resistance. Their experiences of suffering and survival reveal the intersections of gender, violence, and power on a global scale.

The Role of Women as Agents of Change

Despite the overwhelming odds, women in conflict zones have always been at the forefront of resistance movements, humanitarian efforts, and peacebuilding initiatives. In many cases, it is women who bear the brunt of suffering, yet they are also the ones who often lead efforts for survival and change. These women are not mere victims; they are warriors, advocates, and leaders in their communities.

In countries like Syria, Iraq, and Afghanistan, women have organized in the face of occupation, war, and displacement. They have fought for the right to education, the right to be heard, and the right to participate in the rebuilding of their societies. In the aftermath of conflict, women often play crucial roles in rebuilding communities, not just physically but socially and culturally. They bring new perspectives to peace negotiations, demand accountability for war crimes, and challenge traditional gender roles that have been reinforced by violence.

Consider the stories of women like Nadia Murad, a Yazidi survivor of ISIS captivity, who has become a global advocate for survivors of sexual violence. Or the women who have led grassroots efforts to bring justice to women subjected to wartime rape in countries like the Democratic Republic of Congo. These women, though scarred by violence, embody the core principles of feminism: resistance to oppression, solidarity with others, and a refusal to accept injustice.

Displacement and Feminism: A Double Burden

Displacement—whether caused by war, political instability, or environmental disaster—is one of the greatest threats to women's rights in the 21st century. Refugees face a complex web of vulnerabilities: they often live in overcrowded, unsanitary camps where resources are scarce, and their movements are restricted. In such environments, women are particularly at risk.

The gendered dimensions of displacement are stark. Women and girls are more likely to suffer from gender-based violence, including sexual assault and domestic violence. They often face barriers to accessing healthcare and education, and in many cases, they are forced into early marriages or coerced into sexual exploitation as a means of survival. Refugee camps, designed to house people temporarily, frequently fail to meet the long-term needs of women, leaving them in a state of perpetual vulnerability.

Yet, amid this chaos, women have also organized for their rights. In refugee camps across the globe, women have established networks to support one another, advocate for better conditions, and demand the protection of their rights. Whether through informal grassroots initiatives or formal organizations, displaced women have formed strong bonds of solidarity. They provide emotional support, fight for access to resources, and demand that their needs be met in the face of international neglect.

Women as Global Feminist Leaders

The struggle of women in crisis zones transcends borders, offering a powerful reminder that the feminist movement is global, and that struggles for justice are interconnected. The women who survive war, displacement, and violence become leaders in their own right, often pushing the boundaries of what is considered "traditional" feminism. They have led movements in their own countries, and many have taken their activism to international platforms.

International organizations, such as the United Nations and NGOs, have increasingly recognized the importance of including women in peace processes and humanitarian aid efforts. Yet, there remains a significant gap between the rhetoric of inclusion and the reality on the ground. Women who are most affected by conflict are often excluded from decision-making processes, their voices drowned out by the political interests of states or international organizations. Feminist leaders and activists continue to call for greater inclusion, not just as beneficiaries of aid, but as decision-makers, negotiators, and agents of change.

Feminist scholars have long argued that the principles of feminism—equity, justice, and the dismantling of power structures—must extend to the global stage. As we consider the challenges faced by women in crisis zones, we must confront uncomfortable truths: war, displacement, and political instability are not just distant realities; they are a direct result of global inequalities, power dynamics, and patriarchal structures that affect women across the world.

Connecting Global Struggles with Feminist Principles

The feminist movement must recognize that the fight for gender equality is not confined to the struggles faced by women in "stable" countries. Instead, the challenges women face in conflict zones and refugee camps must be central to feminist discourse. Feminism must respond to the unique needs of women in crisis and support their efforts to lead change in their communities. It is not enough for the movement to focus solely on gender equality within the context of Western, middle-class experiences. The global struggle for women's rights must include the voices of those who have been displaced, marginalized, and oppressed in the most extreme ways.

In this chapter, we connect the feminist principles of equity, justice, and resistance to the stories of women who live on the margins of global conflict. These women, through their courage, resilience, and leadership, demonstrate the power of feminism to transcend borders, challenging not just local oppressions, but global systems of inequality. Feminism in crisis zones is not a passive response to suffering, but an active, ongoing struggle for liberation—one that calls for solidarity and action, both locally and globally.

Conclusion: Feminism's Global Duty

The crisis faced by women in conflict zones and refugee camps is a critical moment for the feminist movement. As we continue to build a more inclusive, intersectional feminism, we must ensure that the experiences of women in crisis are not just acknowledged, but prioritized. These women represent the heart of feminist action: they refuse to be silenced, they fight for their rights, and they push for change in the face of unimaginable adversity.

The global feminist movement has a responsibility to amplify their voices, support their leadership, and demand that their struggles be recognized as central to the fight for justice and equality. Only through this global solidarity can we begin to build a world where women, regardless of their circumstances, have the freedom, security, and agency to shape their own futures.

CHAPTER 8

Health Disparities: Fighting for Bodily Autonomy

Health is not simply a matter of physical well-being; it is a powerful indicator of societal structures, privileges, and inequalities. For many women, especially those in marginalized communities, health disparities are not just about lack of access to care—they are about systemic neglect, denial of autonomy, and the erosion of their most basic rights. In this chapter, we dive into the intersection of health and feminism, focusing on how healthcare access, reproductive rights, and mental health challenges are deeply tied to the fight for gender equality and justice. The inequalities faced by women in health aren't isolated problems—they are fundamental to the fight for autonomy, equity, and freedom.

The Crisis of Maternal Mortality

One of the most glaring and deadly health disparities is maternal mortality. Around the world, particularly in low-income and marginalized communities, women die at alarming rates during childbirth, often due to preventable conditions. In the United States, Black women are three to four times more likely to die from pregnancy-related complications than white women, regardless of income or education level. This staggering statistic speaks to the intersection of race, class, and gender, where systemic racism, inadequate healthcare, and lack of access to resources combine to create a deadly reality for many women.

But the maternal mortality crisis is not confined to the U.S.; it is a global issue, with women in impoverished regions of Africa, Latin America, and Asia facing similar risks. Poor healthcare infrastructure, lack of trained medical personnel, and limited access to prenatal and postnatal care are among the root causes of this crisis. However, the problem extends beyond just healthcare access—it is a matter of autonomy. In many societies, women's health, especially reproductive health, is often dictated by cultural and political forces that view women's bodies as objects of control rather than agents of their own choices.

Feminists advocating for reproductive rights and health equity have long argued that bodily autonomy is a cornerstone of gender equality. The ability to make decisions about one's body, including decisions about pregnancy and childbirth, is essential to a woman's agency. Without access to safe and affordable maternal care, and without the power to make decisions about her reproductive health, a woman's freedom is severely restricted.

The Battle for Abortion Rights

Abortion is one of the most contentious issues in feminist discourse, yet it is fundamentally about a woman's right to control her own body. The ongoing political battles over abortion rights in the United States, as well as in countries around the world, highlight the stark inequalities women face when it comes to reproductive autonomy. The criminalization of abortion and the stigmatization of women who seek it disproportionately affect marginalized groups—especially low-income women, women of color, and young women.

When abortion is illegal or heavily restricted, it is often the most vulnerable women who bear the brunt of the consequences. They are forced to travel long distances to find safe procedures or resort to unsafe methods that put their lives at risk. Even when abortion is legal, access remains an issue, as women in rural or underserved areas may face significant barriers to obtaining services. The cost of the procedure, insurance coverage, and logistical barriers often leave women with fewer options than they should have in a society that claims to value equality.

Reproductive justice advocates argue that the fight for abortion rights is not just about the right to terminate a pregnancy, but about the broader issue of reproductive autonomy. The right to choose how and when to have children is a fundamental component of gender equality. Without this autonomy, women are denied control over their futures, trapped in cycles of poverty, and forced to bear the consequences of a system that fails to prioritize their well-being.

Mental Health: The Silent Struggle

Mental health is another crucial aspect of health equity that is often overlooked in feminist discussions. Women in marginalized communities—whether they are living in poverty, experiencing domestic violence, or facing systemic racism—are more likely to suffer from mental health challenges, yet they have less access to the care they need. The stigma surrounding mental health, combined with a lack of culturally competent services, often leaves women of color, LGBTQ+ individuals, and low-income women without the support they need.

Moreover, the intersectionality of gender, race, and class compounds mental health struggles. Women who experience multiple forms of marginalization, such as Black women or transgender women, are at a higher risk of developing mental health issues due to the cumulative stress of discrimination, violence, and oppression. The trauma they experience is not only individual but societal, shaped by deeply ingrained power dynamics that dictate their worth, safety, and well-being.

Feminist mental health advocates argue for a more inclusive and holistic approach to mental health, one that considers the unique experiences of marginalized women. It is not enough to provide generic mental health care—it must be culturally sensitive, trauma-informed, and accessible to all. Moreover, mental health care should be seen as a right, not a luxury. A woman's ability to thrive in her life, her work, and her relationships is intrinsically linked to her mental health, and this is a feminist issue that demands attention.

Bodily Autonomy: The Feminist Demand for Health Equity

Bodily autonomy—defined as the right to make decisions about one's own body—is the core issue uniting all of the health disparities we have discussed. Whether it is a woman's right to choose abortion, to access prenatal care, or to seek mental health services, bodily autonomy is central to her freedom. For marginalized women, this autonomy is frequently denied, whether through systemic barriers to care, cultural expectations, or outright legal restrictions. The feminist movement has always championed the right to bodily autonomy, and this fight must continue on all fronts.

Health equity is not just about providing access to medical services—it is about dismantling the systems that perpetuate inequality and prevent marginalized women from making informed, autonomous choices about their bodies. Feminist advocacy must focus on challenging the power structures that control women's access to health care, while also creating spaces where women's health needs are understood, respected, and prioritized.

Conclusion: The Intersection of Health and Feminism

As we fight for gender equality, we must confront the harsh reality of health disparities faced by marginalized women. Reproductive rights, maternal health, mental health, and bodily autonomy are not peripheral issues—they are at the heart of feminist advocacy. The denial of access to adequate healthcare and the infringement on women's autonomy are forms of systemic oppression that must be addressed in the pursuit of justice.

The fight for health equity is a feminist fight. It is a fight for every woman's right to control her own body, make decisions about her health, and live free from violence and discrimination. The feminist movement must continue to push for policies and practices that ensure all women, regardless of race, class, or background, have access to the care they need to live healthy, fulfilling lives. Only then can we truly claim a world where gender equality is not just an aspiration, but a reality.

CHAPTER 9

The Power of Representation

Representation is not just about visibility; it is about power—the power to shape narratives, to influence perceptions, and to reflect the diversity of experiences that make up the human condition. When it comes to feminism, representation matters deeply. The way women are portrayed in media, literature, and pop culture not only influences how we see ourselves but also how the world sees us. For marginalized women—those who do not fit the narrow confines of mainstream representation—visibility is a critical tool in the fight for equality and justice.

This chapter explores the complex relationship between feminism and representation, looking at how media, literature, and pop culture have historically shaped, distorted, or silenced feminist voices. We will delve into the ways in which the lack of diversity in feminist narratives has reinforced a one-dimensional, often whitewashed version of womanhood. And we will celebrate the trailblazers—those who have used their platforms to challenge stereotypes, break barriers, and amplify the voices of women from all walks of life.

The Narrow Lens of Mainstream Representation

Mainstream media has long perpetuated a very specific image of feminism—one that is predominantly white, middle-class, able-bodied, cisgender, and heterosexual. This limited portrayal has shaped public perception of who a feminist is and what feminism represents. The "face" of feminism, as seen in magazines, movies, and television shows, has often been a thin, white woman in a well-paying job, advocating for issues that align with the experiences of this specific demographic. While these representations are valid for some, they ignore the complexities and challenges faced by women who exist on the margins.

For many women of color, working-class women, disabled women, and LGBTQ+ individuals, mainstream feminist narratives can feel alienating or even hostile. The lack of representation in the media not only erases their struggles but also dismisses their contributions to feminist movements. The voices and stories of these women are frequently left out of the broader feminist discourse, and their experiences are often overshadowed by the struggles of more privileged groups.

When women of color, for example, are depicted in media, they are often confined to stereotypical roles—submissive, exoticized, or portrayed as angry and irrational. These portrayals do not allow for the full expression of their humanity or the complexities of their identities. Similarly, LGBTQ+ women face marginalization within feminist spaces, with their experiences of gender identity, sexuality, and oppression rarely reflected in mainstream feminist narratives.

Breaking the Silence: Diverse Voices in Feminism

Despite the overwhelming dominance of a white, middle-class feminist image, there has always been a rich history of diverse women contributing to feminist thought and activism. Black feminists, Indigenous feminists, and feminists of the global South have long critiqued the limitations of mainstream feminism, offering alternative frameworks that center race, class, and colonialism as integral parts of the struggle for gender justice. Figures like Audre Lorde, bell hooks, Kimberlé Crenshaw, and Gloria Anzaldúa have provided vital contributions to feminist thought, emphasizing the importance of intersectionality and the need for a feminism that is inclusive of all women.

The feminist movement, in its many forms, has always thrived on the margins. But it is only in recent years that more diverse voices have gained prominence in mainstream media and pop culture. Writers like Roxane Gay and Chimamanda Ngozi Adichie, filmmakers like Ava DuVernay and Lulu Wang, and activists like Tarana Burke and Alicia Garza have challenged the status quo and created space for women who have historically been excluded. Through their work, they have shown that feminism is not a monolith—it is a movement that is as diverse as the women it seeks to empower.

These women are rewriting the narrative of feminism, offering more complex, nuanced, and authentic portrayals of what it means to be a woman in today's world. They highlight the realities of being a Black woman, a queer woman, a disabled woman, or an immigrant woman, all while challenging the stereotypes and assumptions that have long defined the feminist agenda. Their voices are breaking through the silence, demanding that the feminist movement reflect the full spectrum of women's experiences.

Media's Role in Shaping Feminist Narratives

The role of media in shaping feminist narratives cannot be overstated. Media is one of the most powerful tools for shaping public perception, and it has the ability to either reinforce or challenge societal norms. In the context of feminism, media has the power to amplify diverse voices or to silence them completely.

The feminist movement has long struggled with being misrepresented or co-opted by mainstream media. Feminist ideals have often been distorted, trivialized, or packaged in ways that strip them of their radical potential. For instance, the "girl power" movement of the 1990s, which was popularized by the Spice Girls and later commercialized by mainstream brands, sometimes seemed more about personal empowerment than systemic change. While personal empowerment is important, it often does not address the structural inequalities that are central to feminist advocacy.

In contrast, the rise of social media and digital platforms has provided a more democratic space for feminist voices. Platforms like Twitter, Instagram, and YouTube have allowed marginalized voices to reach global audiences, creating new spaces for grassroots activism and feminist expression. Hashtags like #BlackLivesMatter, #MeToo, and #SayHerName have sparked global conversations about race, gender, and sexual violence, showing the power of social media to challenge dominant narratives and create spaces for marginalized women to speak out.

The Importance of Authentic Feminist Representation

The demand for authentic representation in feminist media is not just about numbers—it's about ensuring that the stories told are accurate, nuanced, and inclusive. Representation must go beyond tokenism or the inclusion of a few diverse faces. It must involve the full inclusion of diverse voices in the writing, directing, and producing processes. When women of color, LGBTQ+ women, and disabled women are given the space to tell their own stories, they can provide a richer, more complex picture of what it means to be a woman in the modern society.

Authentic representation allows marginalized women to see themselves reflected in stories that validate their experiences and challenges. It affirms their right to exist, to be heard, and to have their struggles recognized. It also provides a model for younger generations of women who may feel alienated by mainstream narratives. Representation helps young girls and women envision themselves as agents of change, leaders, and activists in their own right.

Feminism, at its core, is about breaking down the systems of power that limit women's lives. To do this, it must be inclusive—not just in its rhetoric but in its practices. The feminist movement must strive for authentic, diverse representation in all aspects of culture, from film and television to literature and politics. Only when all women—regardless of race, class, sexuality, or ability—see themselves reflected in the feminist narrative will we be able to achieve true gender equality.

Conclusion: The Power of Representation in Shaping Feminist Futures

As we look to the future of feminism, the power of representation must remain at the forefront. The voices of marginalized women are not peripheral—they are central to the feminist movement. To build a truly inclusive feminism, we must continue to push for greater representation in media, literature, and pop culture.

The feminist narrative must reflect the diverse experiences, struggles, and triumphs of all women. Only through authentic representation can we create a feminism that is truly transformative—one that dismantles the systems of power that oppress us and uplifts the voices of those who have been silenced for too long. As we move forward, let us celebrate the diversity within the feminist movement and ensure that every woman, regardless of her background or identity, has a place at the table.

CHAPTER 10

Feminism and Allyship: Bridging Divides

In any movement that seeks to challenge entrenched systems of power, the idea of allyship is vital. But allyship is not a passive role—it's an active, ongoing process of solidarity, reflection, and accountability. In the context of feminism, allyship involves those from more privileged backgrounds—be it white, cisgender, able-bodied, or middle-class—using their power and platform to support marginalized voices, without overshadowing or co-opting the struggles of others.

This chapter explores the complex and sometimes controversial role of allyship within feminist activism. It delves into what it means to be an ally, how allyship can be practiced in ways that don't perpetuate the very systems of oppression it seeks to dismantle, and how solidarity can build bridges across divides within the feminist movement.

Understanding Allyship: More Than Just Support

Allyship is often misunderstood as a simple act of support—showing up to a protest, retweeting a feminist post, or offering a kind word. While these acts are valuable, allyship requires a deeper level of engagement. True allyship means using one's privilege not just to amplify voices but to challenge the structures that perpetuate inequality. It's about understanding that privilege isn't just a personal trait, but a social condition that shapes the dynamics of power in society. For those with privilege, allyship involves recognizing this power and actively working to dismantle systems that uphold inequality.

In feminist terms, being an ally means creating spaces for marginalized women—women of color, LGBTQ+ women, disabled women, and working-class women—to speak, while also ensuring that these voices are heard and respected. It means understanding that feminism isn't one-size-fits-all. While the struggles of white women and women of color may share common threads, they are also distinct and shaped by different histories and contexts. Therefore, allyship must be a nuanced, informed, and empathetic practice.

The Dangers of "Performative" Allyship

While allyship is essential, it can easily fall into the trap of performative activism—the act of seeming to support a cause while doing little to actually challenge the systems that sustain oppression. Performative allyship often centers the ally rather than the oppressed, turning the conversation into one about their own "goodness" or "wokeness" rather than the struggles of those they claim to support.

A glaring example of this can be seen in how feminism has sometimes been co-opted by those with privileged backgrounds, turning the movement into a platform for their personal empowerment without recognizing the unique struggles of marginalized women. In many instances, white women have taken center stage in mainstream feminist narratives, speaking over or for women of color. This is particularly dangerous in intersectional spaces, where it's crucial that we lift up the voices of those who are often silenced by society.

To avoid the pitfalls of performative allyship, it's important for allies to be self-reflective and practice humility. It's not about making yourself look good—it's about genuinely listening, learning, and taking action in ways that prioritize marginalized voices and work to shift power dynamics.

The Role of Privileged Women in Feminist Activism

While the feminist movement has been largely driven by women from marginalized backgrounds, it's clear that those with more privilege have a critical role to play in pushing for systemic change. But how do women from privileged backgrounds support feminism without taking over the conversation? How do they ensure that they are not inadvertently silencing the very people they seek to help?

The key lies in creating spaces of shared responsibility—spaces where women from all backgrounds can contribute while recognizing their own positionality within systems of power. For white feminists, for example, the task is not to lead, but to amplify and support the leadership of women of color. For cisgender feminists, it is not to speak for transgender women, but to listen to their needs and support their right to self-determination.

An example of effective allyship can be seen in the feminist movements that have emerged around the world, where women from different backgrounds unite to demand gender justice. These movements often center marginalized voices—especially those who have been excluded from mainstream feminist discourse—and invite allies to participate in ways that support, rather than overshadow, the leadership of the oppressed.

Practical Ways to Practice Allyship

Allyship is an ongoing practice that requires active participation and a commitment to personal and collective transformation. Here are some practical ways that those with privilege can engage in meaningful allyship within feminism:

1 Educate yourself by reading books: going to workshops, and interacting with material that makes you think. of feminism. Learn about the history of marginalized communities and the specific struggles they face. Knowledge is power, and understanding different forms of oppression will better equip you to advocate for change.

2 Listen and Amplify: Rather than speaking over marginalized women, listen to their experiences and amplify their voices. Share their work, platform their ideas, and support their leadership. Instead of responding, listen with the goal of understanding.

3 Support Marginalized Leaders: Step back and allow women from marginalized backgrounds to lead. Offer your resources—be it financial, organizational, or emotional—in ways that empower them without taking the spotlight. Recognize that the leadership of women of color, queer women, and disabled women is essential to a truly inclusive feminist movement.

4 Take Accountability: Allyship requires a commitment to self-reflection. When you make mistakes (and you will), take responsibility and use it as an opportunity to grow. Understand that allyship isn't about perfection—it's about progress.

5 Challenge Your Own Privilege: Recognize the ways in which your privilege may show up in spaces you occupy. Be willing to challenge your own biases and assumptions, even when it feels uncomfortable. True allyship means constantly examining your own actions and adjusting accordingly.

Allyship as Solidarity in Action

Allyship is not just about standing alongside marginalized groups—it's about taking action to transform the structures that perpetuate inequality. Solidarity involves actively working to change systems of power, whether that means advocating for policy reforms, supporting grassroots organizations, or challenging discrimination in your personal and professional life.

Feminism, in its most radical form, aims to dismantle patriarchal structures that uphold all forms of oppression. But this task cannot be accomplished by any one group alone. It requires the collective effort of individuals from all walks of life—particularly those with privilege who have the power to challenge systems of power and support marginalized communities.

When done right, allyship strengthens the feminist movement by creating a united front that transcends individual differences and focuses on the collective goal of gender equality. It is a shared responsibility, one that requires ongoing effort, commitment, and a deep respect for the voices and leadership of those most affected by injustice.

Conclusion: A Feminist Movement of Solidarity

As we continue to push for social, political, and economic change, it is crucial that the feminist movement remains rooted in solidarity. True allyship is not a passive role—it is an active, ongoing process that requires reflection, humility, and commitment. The strength of feminism lies in its inclusivity—its ability to bring together women from all backgrounds, each with their own experiences, to work toward a common goal of justice and equality.

By recognizing the importance of allyship, we can bridge the divides that have historically existed within the feminist movement. When women from privileged backgrounds support marginalized voices and commit to dismantling the systems of power that oppress us, we build a united front that can transform the world. Feminism is not a competition—it's a collective struggle, and in solidarity, we will win

CHAPTER 11

Grassroots Initiatives: Revolution from the Ground Up

Change, in its most enduring form, often begins from the grassroots—among the people, in the communities, and in the spaces that institutional movements have overlooked or neglected. Grassroots feminism is the embodiment of this principle, a movement rooted in everyday activism that challenges the structural inequities women face in their daily lives. It is in these spaces—where women gather in solidarity, often without significant funding or institutional support—that the most transformative changes can be made.

This chapter explores the power of grassroots movements in advancing feminist causes, particularly in marginalized communities. It highlights the significance of localized, community-driven initiatives, and how they have not only responded to the needs of these communities but have also created ripple effects that inspire national and global change. We'll delve into real-world examples of successful campaigns led by women in the margins, and we'll explore how their work can serve as a blueprint for fostering feminism from the ground up.

The Power of Community-Based Feminism

Grassroots movements are characterized by their deeply localized nature. They arise organically from within communities, driven by those who experience the challenges firsthand. For feminist movements, this means addressing the specific issues women face in their everyday lives—issues often ignored by larger, more centralized feminist organizations. Whether it's fighting for safe drinking water, challenging domestic violence, or demanding better healthcare, grassroots feminists are the ones most in touch with the lived realities of marginalized women.

One of the defining features of grassroots movements is their ability to create change without relying on traditional power structures. They are often fueled by the energy, creativity, and resilience of women who have been excluded from mainstream channels of influence. These movements don't wait for permission or recognition from larger organizations—they create their own spaces, fight for their own needs, and build their own networks of solidarity. This has allowed them to resist co-optation by powerful institutions and to remain true to the needs of the people they serve.

Grassroots feminism is not about top-down, one-size-fits-all solutions—it's about empowering communities to shape their own futures. In these spaces, women find strength in collective action and mutual support, and they learn to demand their rights, not as a form of protest, but as a fundamental part of their dignity and self-worth.

Case Studies of Successful Grassroots Feminist Movements

Several notable grassroots campaigns have illustrated how effective community-based feminism can be. These movements, though often underreported in mainstream media, have had profound impacts on their communities and beyond.

One example is the **Black Lives Matter** movement, which, while centered on racial justice, also incorporates a strong feminist perspective. Founded by women of color, the movement highlights the intersecting struggles of Black women, who experience both racial and gendered violence. Through local chapters and community initiatives, Black Lives Matter has worked to build networks of support for marginalized women, advocating for everything from police accountability to access to healthcare.

Another powerful example is the "**Ni Una Menos**" movement in Argentina, which began as a grassroots campaign against femicide and violence against women. The movement rapidly spread throughout Latin America, driven by the stories of women who faced violence and systemic injustice. Through marches, protests, and digital campaigns, Ni Una Menos has forced governments to take action on gender violence and femicide, demonstrating how grassroots activism can push for legislative change.

In India, the "**Bharatiya Mahila Federation**" (Indian Women's Federation) works to empower rural women through education, health initiatives, and political organizing. This community-driven approach has enabled women in remote areas to not only fight for their rights but also gain control over their economic and political lives. The Federation has been instrumental in advocating for women's labor rights, combating sexual violence, and providing women with the tools to become agents of change in their communities.

These movements, and many others like them, show that when communities take ownership of their struggles, they are better able to address their specific needs, foster long-term change, and build solidarity across borders.

Feminism from the Margins: The Role of Marginalized Women in Grassroots Movements

Marginalized women are often the catalysts behind grassroots feminist movements. They have the lived experience that informs their activism, and their struggles are inherently intersectional. These women know firsthand what it means to fight against multiple forms of oppression, whether it's based on race, class, ability, or sexuality. For many of them, the fight for gender justice is inextricably tied to struggles for racial justice, economic equality, or environmental sustainability.

In marginalized communities, feminist movements do not look the same as they do in more privileged spaces. They are often deeply community-focused, shaped by the cultural, social, and economic conditions that women face. In these spaces, feminist activism often intersects with other forms of advocacy, such as labor movements, environmental justice, or anti-colonial struggles. The result is a form of feminism that is more comprehensive, inclusive, and responsive to the realities of those on the margins.

Take, for example, the work of Indigenous women in Canada, where the issue of Missing and Murdered Indigenous Women (MMIW) has sparked a national grassroots movement. Indigenous women have led efforts to raise awareness about the epidemic of violence against their sisters, pushing for justice while also advocating for cultural sovereignty, land rights, and the preservation of Indigenous ways of life. These movements are driven by Indigenous feminists who blend gender advocacy with resistance against colonialism and environmental destruction. Their fight is both personal and collective, challenging the historical and contemporary forces that oppress them.

How to Support or Start a Grassroots Feminist Initiative

Supporting grassroots movements requires more than just donating money or showing up to rallies. It involves understanding the unique needs of the communities you wish to support and being willing to engage in long-term work that prioritizes their leadership.

If you're considering starting a grassroots feminist initiative, here are some key principles to guide your efforts:

1. Start with the community: Grassroots movements should always begin with the community's needs. Take time to listen and understand the challenges they face. Build relationships of trust and respect before jumping into action.

2. Empower local leadership: It's essential that those who are directly impacted by the issues you're addressing are given leadership roles in the movement. The best solutions come from those who have lived the struggles.

3. Be intersectional: Recognize the ways in which race, class, sexuality, and other factors intersect to create unique forms of oppression. Grassroots feminism should be inclusive of all women, regardless of their background or identity.

4. Utilize local resources: Often, grassroots initiatives don't require large amounts of funding—they require ingenuity, collaboration, and the willingness to work within local resources.

5. Keep the momentum going: Grassroots movements can face immense challenges, including burnout, funding shortages, and resistance from larger systems. It's important to stay connected to the community and keep your focus on long-term goals.

Conclusion: Building Feminist Movements from the Ground Up

Grassroots movements are the lifeblood of feminist activism. They not only challenge existing power structures but also provide an avenue for those most affected by injustice to reclaim their agency and power. By supporting or starting grassroots initiatives, we can help build a more inclusive, localized feminist movement—one that operates from the ground up, prioritizes marginalized voices, and works toward systemic change.

As we continue to push for gender justice, we must remember that the most enduring change often comes from the community level. In these spaces, women have the power to reshape their lives, their families, and their societies. Feminism, when rooted in the community, can grow from the margins to the center, creating a movement that is truly global, intersectional, and transformative.

Chapter 12

Building an Inclusive Future

As we conclude this journey through the complexities of intersectional feminism, it's clear that the feminist movement is at a pivotal moment. The movement we've discussed here is not simply one of theory or abstract ideals—it's a call to action, one that demands we move beyond the confines of mainstream feminism and embrace a more inclusive, holistic vision that centers the voices and experiences of those too often silenced or erased. This is a vision where feminism doesn't just belong to a select few, but to every woman, regardless of race, class, sexuality, ability, or geography.

But understanding the issues is only the beginning. The true challenge lies in translating that knowledge into action. Now that we've explored the foundations of intersectionality, examined the struggles of marginalized women, and recognized the power of grassroots movements, we must consider what we, as individuals and communities, can do to create a future where feminism is truly inclusive, accessible, and transformative for all.

Key Lessons from the Book

Throughout this book, we've explored the myriad ways in which feminism must evolve to meet the needs of marginalized women. Here are some key takeaways:

1. Intersectionality is essential: We cannot talk about feminism without acknowledging the ways in which race, class, gender, sexuality, and other factors intersect to create complex systems of oppression. Feminism needs to be intersectional in order to effectively address the distinct experiences of every woman.

2. Mainstream feminism needs to be more inclusive: For too long, mainstream feminism has been dominated by the voices and experiences of middle-class white women. We've seen how this narrow lens has excluded marginalized women and LGBTQ+ individuals, failing to address their unique struggles. To build a truly inclusive movement, we must listen to, support, and amplify the voices of those on the margins.

3. Grassroots activism is the heart of change: The most transformative feminist movements often begin in the grassroots—among local communities who are already organizing and advocating for their rights. These movements may be small, but they are powerful. They are often led by women who have the lived experience and the passion to drive real change.

4. Cultural and social structures shape gender oppression: From patriarchal norms to colonial legacies, cultural traditions and social structures heavily influence the ways in which women are oppressed. Feminism must find ways to navigate these complexities without erasing identities, traditions, or cultural practices that empower women.

5. We all have a role to play: Whether you are directly affected by these issues or not, we all have a role in building an inclusive feminist movement. Feminism is a movement for everyone, not just a select few. We must all take responsibility for creating change, both within our communities and in the larger world.

What Can You Do?

Now that we've explored the need for a more inclusive and intersectional feminist movement, the question remains: What can you, as a reader, do to help build this future? The answer lies in both reflection and action. The steps you take may seem small at first, but when multiplied by thousands or millions of people, these actions can create the tidal wave of change that we need. Here are some practical steps you can take:

1. Listen and Learn: To truly support marginalized women, we must first listen to them. Learn about the struggles they face, whether through books, documentaries, or conversations with people from different communities. Prioritize learning from voices that are often unheard. Understand that their struggles are not isolated but are part of larger systems of power and oppression.

2. Amplify Marginalized Voices: If you are in a position of privilege, use it to uplift the voices of those who are often silenced. Amplify the work of women of color, disabled women, queer women, and others whose contributions are often overlooked. Share their stories, center their work, and provide platforms where their voices can be heard.

3. Support Grassroots Movements: Whether through financial donations, volunteer work, or spreading awareness, supporting grassroots movements is one of the most effective ways to help build an inclusive feminist future. These movements are often underfunded and overlooked, but they are the ones creating real, lasting change. Find local or global movements that align with your values and lend them your support.

4. Challenge Systems of Oppression: Intersectional feminism isn't just about recognizing inequalities—it's about challenging the systems that perpetuate them. Whether it's in your workplace, community, or government, advocate for policies that address gender-based violence, wage disparities, reproductive rights, and healthcare access. Hold those in power accountable, and demand that they act with justice and equity.

5. Reflect on Your Own Biases: No one is exempt from the work of self-reflection. Challenge your own assumptions, biases, and privileges. Recognize the ways in which your own identity may influence how you perceive or act toward others. This is a continual process of growth and change, but it is necessary if we are to build a truly inclusive feminist movement.

6. Foster Solidarity and Allyship: Feminism isn't a competition—it's about solidarity. Allies play a critical role in advocating for marginalized groups, but it's important to recognize that allyship is not about being the loudest voice in the room; it's about stepping aside when necessary and letting the affected voices lead. Solidarity means supporting others in their struggles, and working together to dismantle systems of oppression.

7. Engage in Activism in Your Own Space: Whether through organizing events, educating others, or simply having difficult conversations, activism can take many forms. You don't have to be part of a large-scale movement to make an impact. Every conversation, every action counts. Use your position to advocate for change in your personal and professional spheres.

9

The Future of Feminism

As we look ahead to the future of feminism, the path forward is clear: the movement must continue to evolve, embracing the voices of those who have been silenced for far too long. Feminism must be intersectional, inclusive, and rooted in solidarity, and it must always seek to dismantle the systems of oppression that hold back marginalized women.

The work we do today, the actions we take, and the conversations we have will shape the feminist movements of tomorrow. But to create real, lasting change, we must keep pushing forward, driven by the belief that a better, more just world is possible. A world where all women, regardless of their background, their identity, or their circumstances, can thrive and live free from the constraints of oppression.

Now, it's your turn. The movement for inclusive feminism is not something that happens in isolation—it requires all of us. It is time for each of us to take our place in this journey. The echoes of those who have been silenced for so long are rising, and it's up to us to listen, to act, and to build the future they deserve.

Conclusion

It is not enough to simply understand the issues; we must actively work to dismantle the systems of oppression that perpetuate them. The task ahead may be daunting, but with solidarity, courage, and a commitment to intersectionality, we can build a world where feminism is truly for everyone. The time to act is now. Let's build the inclusive future we all deserve.

Made in the USA
Middletown, DE
14 March 2025